Mt Ngauruhoe

volcanic and
thermal
New Zealand

Mud pools, Waiotapu

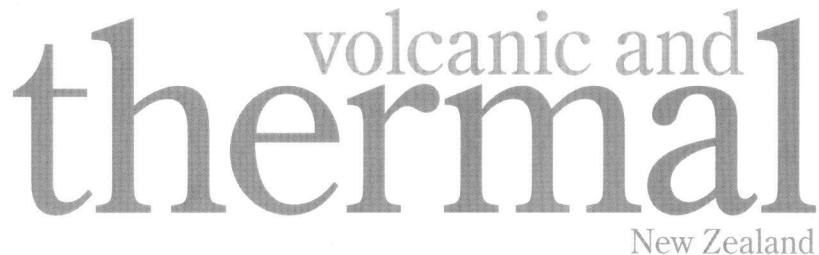

volcanic and thermal

New Zealand

TREVERN & ANNA DAWES

PENGUIN

VIKING

'The sight that met our view was truly appalling . . . the black cloud was
rent in two and an immense sheet of flame shot up thousands of feet into the
air, and then the red-hot stones and cinders rolled down the sides of the
mountain . . . In the early part of the eruption, lightning seemed to pass from
the bowels of the earth on the outskirts of the gradually expanding cloud in
every direction, thousands of brilliant electric sparks appeared and then
disappeared again behind the dense volumes of cloud and smoke reminding one of
a splendid display of fireworks. This was followed by lightning in every
known form – forked, chain and sheet in rapid succession. The heavens were
one continuous crack and roar.'

Land Court Judge Henry Tacy Clarke's description of the Mt Tarawera eruption, 10 June 1886.

Mt Tarawera with Mt Edgecumbe in the distance

The volcanic crater of Mt Eden and the city of Auckland

Introduction

Planet Earth consists of an interlocking set of rigid plates on a fluid core. Plate movement may be measured in millimetres per year, but when collisions eventuate, molten rock will often break through fractures to form new volcanoes or activate existing ones. The westward-moving Pacific Plate strikes the Indo-Australian Plate at the Hikurangi Trench, about a hundred kilometres to the east of New Zealand. Earthquakes capable of penetration under the western side of New Zealand to a depth of 250 kilometres are created as the Pacific Plate is forced downwards. Although earthquakes are reasonably common in New Zealand, they are not as frequent, nor are they as destructive, as in other places on the Pacific Rim.

The volcanic and associated thermal features of New Zealand form part of the Pacific Ring of Fire or circum-Pacific seismic belt, a vast, horseshoe-shaped area extending to the rim of the Pacific Ocean. Remnants of activity are broadly spread throughout New Zealand, but the active and potentially active central zone is concentrated in the North Island from White Island, through Rotorua and down to Tongariro National Park. This region is known as the Taupo Volcanic Zone.

Geothermal systems are commonly associated with young volcanic zones. When rainwater percolates down to sources of heat it becomes a hot mineral-rich fluid. Hot water is less dense than cold water and where it can find a way back to the surface it can discharge in explosive geysers, fumaroles (gas vents) and mud pools, or, more sedately, via hot springs. The span of these water cycles can vary from a few to tens of thousands of years.

Geothermal water carries a variety of suspended chemical compounds. As the water cools, a chemical sediment of sinter, mostly in the form of silica, is slowly deposited in soils or on rock terraces and can combine with algal growth to add further colourisation.

Although steam may initially have been a welcome source of energy in the city of Rotorua, it did have an adverse effect on geothermal activity in the area. Today, in order to protect the geyser areas and their tourist appeal, the use of steam for domestic purposes has been significantly reduced and controlled.

The country's largest natural heat flow lies further south in the Wairakei–Taupo region. Here bores have been drilled to harness the potential of this vast geothermal field. Steam is removed from the steam and water mix and piped to a power station where turbines generate electricity for the national grid.

Volcanoes, silica terraces, mud pools, geysers, pumice ash, lava flows and domes are all remnants of a turbulent volcanic history. Today these features can be seen at White Island, Hells Gate/Tikitere, Te Puia, Mt Tarawera, Waimangu, Waiotapu, Orakei Korako, Wairakei and Tongariro National Park.

All of these areas are accessible to the public, either as a part of organised commercial tours or as self-guided walks. Some locations are enclosed within relatively small reserves, while others require a fair amount of walking within Tongariro National Park. Many prominent features have been given fanciful or sinister English names, such as the Emerald Terrace, Champagne Pool, Sodom and Gomorrah, and the Devil's Throat. Maori history and legends also relate to these features and add another dimension of significance to these fascinating areas.

As well as the Taupo Volcanic Zone, there are many other volcanic and thermal remnants scattered throughout New Zealand in areas as far north as Kaikohe in Northland and as far south as the Copeland River near Fox Glacier in the South Island. Mt Egmont/Taranaki, an almost perfectly symmetrical classic cone on a flat plain, lies well to the west. Auckland has about fifty small volcanic mountains, while Lyttelton and Otago harbours and their associated peninsulas in the South Island all have volcanic histories.

Waikite Valley, the largest single source of boiling water in New Zealand

White Island

White Island, the emergent summit of a submarine volcano, lies 50 kilometres offshore in the Bay of Plenty. Although not directly connected to the North Island volcanic cluster dominated by Ruapehu, White Island provides a convenient safety valve to that system. Known to the Maori as Whakaari (that which can be made visible), the island only appears sharp on the horizon on very clear days. Although the volcano is estimated to be between 100 000 and 200 000 years old, it has an 'island' presence of only 2.7 kilometres in length and 1.5 kilometres in width, with its highest point of 321 metres at Mt Gisborne only dating back 16 000 years.

Lieutenant (later Captain) James Cook, after rounding East Cape on 31 October 1769 in the *Endeavour*, recorded in his log: 'The land seen yesterday bearing west and which we now saw was an island bore SW distant 8 leagues. I have named it White Island because as such it always appear'd to us.' The contemporary observer, however, might prefer the more colourful legend of Maui, the Maori hero who is said to have created the island by flinging fire into the sea.

Lava from volcanic eruptions usually hardens to seal vents and fumaroles. This is followed by a dormant period during which pressure accumulates to create the next eruption. However, a continuous release of pressure can occur as a result of large areas of the rock surface being eroded by streams of acid.

Vast areas of acidic mud and water, innumerable fumaroles, and gas circulated by unpredictable winds make White Island an extremely inhospitable place. Since 1826 significant steam and ash eruptions have been recorded on thirty occasions. This volatile landscape of fumaroles, hot springs and vents is subject to change at any time.

Sulphur was first mined on the island in 1885, but this operation was later abandoned in the early 1900s. A second effort commenced in 1913 and was promptly concluded following a landslide in 1914 that killed eleven people and destroyed the buildings on the island. Production was resumed in 1923 and continued until the Depression, when bankruptcy forced closure once more. Since then, the island has seen no further commercial mining because of the hostile nature of the environment.

White Island is privately owned and has had a 'Private Scenic Reserve' status since the early 1950s. Access is strictly controlled to ensure the safe supervision of visitors.

White Island

Southern approach to White Island

Eastern perspective of White Island

White Island's main crater

White Island's main crater

Sulphur deposits, White Island

Mud pools and sulphur deposits, White Island

Mining relics, White Island

Tour group on eastern side of White Island

Rotorua

Rotorua introduces itself to its visitors in no uncertain terms with its pungent odour of hydrogen sulphide. The city has been variously described as 'Sulphur City', 'Stinkville' and 'Rotten Egg Town'. The local Maori seem to have been no less charitable: the area around the Government Gardens is known as Whangapiro, meaning 'an evil smelling place'.

This resort city is best known for its association with thermal activity in New Zealand. Apart from the local private and public thermal swimming pools and spas, there are four main thermal spring attractions in the area – Rainbow Springs, Fairy Springs, Taniwha Springs and Paradise Valley.

The local area's main attraction is Te Puia – guardians of the Whakarewarewa Thermal Valley. Here is located the only major geyser field left in New Zealand. Hundreds of geysers and chloride springs are set within a ring of semi-stagnant, acidic sulphate ponds and mud pools. The highlight is Geyser Flat, where well known Pohutu, Prince of Wales Feathers, Kereru, and Waikorohihi geysers play. The Prince of Wales Feathers erupts to a height of about 12 metres, and either accompanies or precedes Pohutu, the largest, which plays an average of fourteen times a day to a height of approximately 18 metres. Pohutu, one of the world's three most famous geysers, has been known to reach heights of up to 30 metres.

Hells Gate, just 15 kilometres to the north-east, provides a contrast to Whakarewarewa. With its myriad of steaming fumaroles, violent boiling springs, eerie sulphur vents, a mud volcano, and the thermal Kakahi Falls, Hells Gate is Rotorua's most active geothermal area. A sinister atmosphere envelops the area, especially on wet, gloomy days, and this is echoed in the use of names like the Devil's Throat, Sodom and Gomorrah, and The Inferno. As George Bernard Shaw reputedly remarked, it is an opportunity to '. . . get close to Hades and yet be able to return'.

In Maori legend the famous warrior Rangi-te-aorere was presented with a beautiful, high-ranking bride called Huritini. When he later became disenchanted with married life, Huritini, in shame and despair at his rejection, plunged into the mud pool that now bears her name. The name Tikitere for the geothermal area was inspired by the wording of her family's lament, following the news of Huritini's death.

Ngamokaiakoko mud pool, Whakarewarewa

Ngaratuatara cooking pool, Whakarewarewa

Pohutu geyser, Whakarewarewa

The Wai Ora pool, Hells Gate

Koro Koro hot lake, Hells Gate

Hells Gate

Mud volcano, Hells Gate

Hot pools, Hells Gate

Stream deposits, Hells Gate

Mud pool near Wai Ora, Hells Gate

Bubbling pool, Hells Gate

Mt Tarawera

New Zealand's most violent and destructive volcanic explosion since European occupation occurred at Mt Tarawera on 10 June 1886.

Nine days before the cataclysmic event, tourists returning by boat from the Pink and White Terraces believed they saw a phantom canoe in the mist. It may well have been a freak wave created by seismic activity, but the local Maori believed it was a Waka Wairua (a spirit canoe) and an evil omen.

At 12.30 a.m. on that fateful day a series of strong earthquakes shook the mountain. About an hour later there was a small explosion on the north-eastern slopes – and then the mountain blew apart. White incandescent rock and enormous clouds of steam were hurled as high as 10 kilometres into the sky. The south-west side erupted, and a violent explosion produced a line of craters along the mountain top. Then the basin of Lake Rotomahana exploded, sucking out a massive column of steam that hurled mud for many kilometres. Volcanic activity finally ceased at 5.30 a.m. The eruption was heard as far south as Blenheim in the South Island, ash reached Christchurch, and some people in Auckland thought the noise and flashing light to be a Russian attack.

Mt Tarawera's eruption submerged the area in mud and rocks, denuded the landscape, and totally destroyed the famous Pink and White Terraces, rated as the eighth wonder of the world. Settlements of Te Ariki, Moura and Te Wairoa were obliterated by blasts, mud and ash, and more than 150 people perished. The inner part of rhyolite domes, formed by a series of eruptions dating between about 17 000 BC and 1400 AD, were exposed.

The stark and beautiful mountain top remains richly coloured. Pink and grey hues enhance the near vertical walls of the 600-year-old rhyolite domes. Above is white-banded pumice and at the top are layers of red and black basalt. Red colouration is due to the oxidation of iron during lava cooling.

Mt Tarawera (1111 metres) is now dormant. It has become one of New Zealand's most popular volcanic features where tour visitors can gain spectacular aerial views or walk through a dramatic and unforgettable landscape.

Richly coloured crater cliff wall, Mt Tarawera

A crater 'canyon' on Mt Tarawera

The impressive wall of one of the five craters on Mt Tarawera

The view across a crater rim, Mt Tarawera and Lake Rotomahana

A rim area of the main crater, Mt Tarawera

Volcanic rock scree in the main crater, Mt Tarawera

A scree slope in the main crater, Mt Tarawera

The Waimangu Volcanic Valley

The Waimangu Volcanic Valley, the world's newest geothermal area, did not exist before the eruption of Mt Tarawera on 10 June 1886. At that time only a small stream flowed down the Haumi Valley into Lake Rotomahana. Apart from the massive craters left on Mt Tarawera, a line of smaller craters were also created stretching as far as Waimangu. Most of these were eventually inundated by the lake, however several higher level craters remain within what is now the Waimangu Volcanic Valley, about 25 kilometres south of Rotorua. The most prominent are Ruaumoko's Throat (Inferno Crater) and Echo Crater.

Superheated sub-surface water flashing to steam has since caused periodic eruptions in the valley. On 1 April 1917 Frying Pan Flat exploded without warning and two people in a nearby hostel were fatally injured by scalding mud. Echo Crater was enlarged and Frying Pan Lake, or the Waimangu Cauldron as it is known today, was created. Dominated by the steaming, red-streaked Cathedral Rocks, the Waimangu Cauldron at 4.85 hectares is one of the world's largest boiling lakes. Here the surface constantly bubbles as gas is released.

Waimangu Geyser broke out from the north-east end of Echo Crater in late 1900 and continued to erupt intermittently until 1904, with mud being hurled up to 150 metres high. During this period an unexpected and violent explosion on the 30 August 1903 killed four people who had disregarded the guide's warning and ventured too close to the geyser.

Ruaumoko's Throat was formed by the Mt Tarawera eruption. Its grey to pale blue colour is attributed to its depth (30 metres) and its cloudiness to fine particles of silica in suspension. Although steep, scarlet-coloured cliffs enclose the small lake, about every six weeks the water level rises a good 10 metres and overflows into Frying Pan Creek.

There are some remarkable sights in the Waimangu Volcanic Valley – the Southern Crater and Emerald Pool, Echo Crater, Waimangu Cauldron, Ngapuia-o-te-papa, the Waimangu Geyser site, Ruaumoko's Throat, Iodine Pool, Warbrick Terrace and the Steaming Cliffs along the western shore of Lake Rotomahana. All these features are spread down along the valley for a distance of almost 3 kilometres and take about an hour to view.

Cathedral Rocks and Frying Pan Lake, Waimangu Volcanic Valley

Echo Crater and Frying Pan Lake, Waimangu Volcanic Valley

Steam emission, Frying Pan Lake, Waimangu Volcanic Valley

Hot stream, Waimangu Volcanic Valley

Hot stream, Waimangu Volcanic Valley

Rim of the Inferno Crater, Waimangu Volcanic Valley

Inferno Crater, Waimangu Volcanic Valley

Near Warbrick Terrace, Waimangu Volcanic Valley

Warbrick Terrace, Waimangu Volcanic Valley

Waiotapu

Waiotapu (meaning 'sacred waters') is part of a scenic reserve administered by the Department of Conservation and is located 27 kilometres south of Rotorua. Only a small portion of the entire 18-square-kilometre area is open to the public.

Pits, bubbling mud pools, fumaroles, boiling pools, steaming vents and terraces are linked by a series of walkways, boardwalks and lookout points in a compact and highly colourful display.

The Champagne Pool is the undeniable centrepiece. This pool covers about 2000 square metres and is the remnant of a 700-year-old volcanic explosion crater. The temperature of the water at the surface is 74°C. High concentrations of metal sulphides (mostly arsenic, antimony, mercury, gold and silver) account for the bright orange colour of submerged ledges inside the rim. Although viable gold deposits lie beneath the pool, preservation measures for the area will ensure mining never occurs. Adjacent to the Champagne Pool is the Artist's Palette, appropriately named for the orange, yellow, grey and green concentrations of the various elements resident in stagnant pools and rocks.

The Primrose Terraces are spread over an area of 1.2 hectares. This is the largest active formation of its type in New Zealand since the destruction of the Pink and White Terraces by the 1886 Mt Tarawera eruption. Pink, white and gold sinter has been deposited to a depth of about 50 centimetres in a series of small steps sweeping down to the Bridal Veil Falls.

Waiotapu contains the largest area of surface thermal activity of all the hydrothermal areas in the Taupo Volcanic Zone. With its variety of features and ease of access it has become a very popular attraction.

Primrose Terrace, Waiotapu

Artist's Palette, Waiotapu

Artist's Palette, Waiotapu

Champagne Pool, Waiotapu

Champagne Pool, Waiotapu

Bubbles in the Champagne Pool, Waiotapu

Devil's Bath, Waiotapu

Primrose Terrace, Waiotapu

Sinter deposits, Primrose Terrace, Waiotapu

Sinter deposits, Primrose Terrace, Waiotapu

Rainbow Crater, Waiotapu

Orakei Korako

Orakei Korako, 68 kilometres south-west of Rotorua, is generally regarded as the most colourful of New Zealand's thermal areas. It is an isolated area and only accessible by boat across the Waikato River.

The hot springs of the valley flow into Lake Ohakuri, a body of water behind the Ohakuri Dam. When this lake was formed in 1961 to facilitate hydroelectricity, the level of the Waikato River at Orakei Korako was raised by 18 metres. Some 200 alkaline hot springs and seventy geysers, including two of the world's largest, were inundated. Fortunately, the new high water levels stimulated activity further up the valley.

The jade-green Emerald Terrace is adjacent to the lake. Beyond this lies the Golden Fleece Terrace or Te Kapua (the cloud), a massive 40-metre-long, 4.6-metre-high buttress of white silica. This is considered to be the largest formation of its type in the world. The colour of the terrace can vary and is largely influenced by outflow from the Artist's Palette, a 1.4-hectare silica terrace consisting of more than 100 springs and mini geysers. Other local features include the Hochstetter Cauldron, Cascade Terrace and the coral-like formations of the Diamond Geyser, which has been known to play up to a height of 9 metres.

Aladdin's Cave or Ruatapu (sacred cave) is thought to have been created by a volcanic eruption and is one of only two caves known to exist in a geothermal field. At the base of the cave, 38 metres below the entrance, is a hot pool called Waiwhakaata (pool of mirrors). In pre-European times Maori women used the cave as a place of adornment. Orakei Korako, meaning 'a place of adorning', takes its name from this custom.

Rainbow Terrace, Orakei Korako

Emerald Terrace, Orakei Korako

Emerald Terrace, Orakei Korako

Artist's Palette, Orakei Korako

Artist's Palette, Orakei Korako

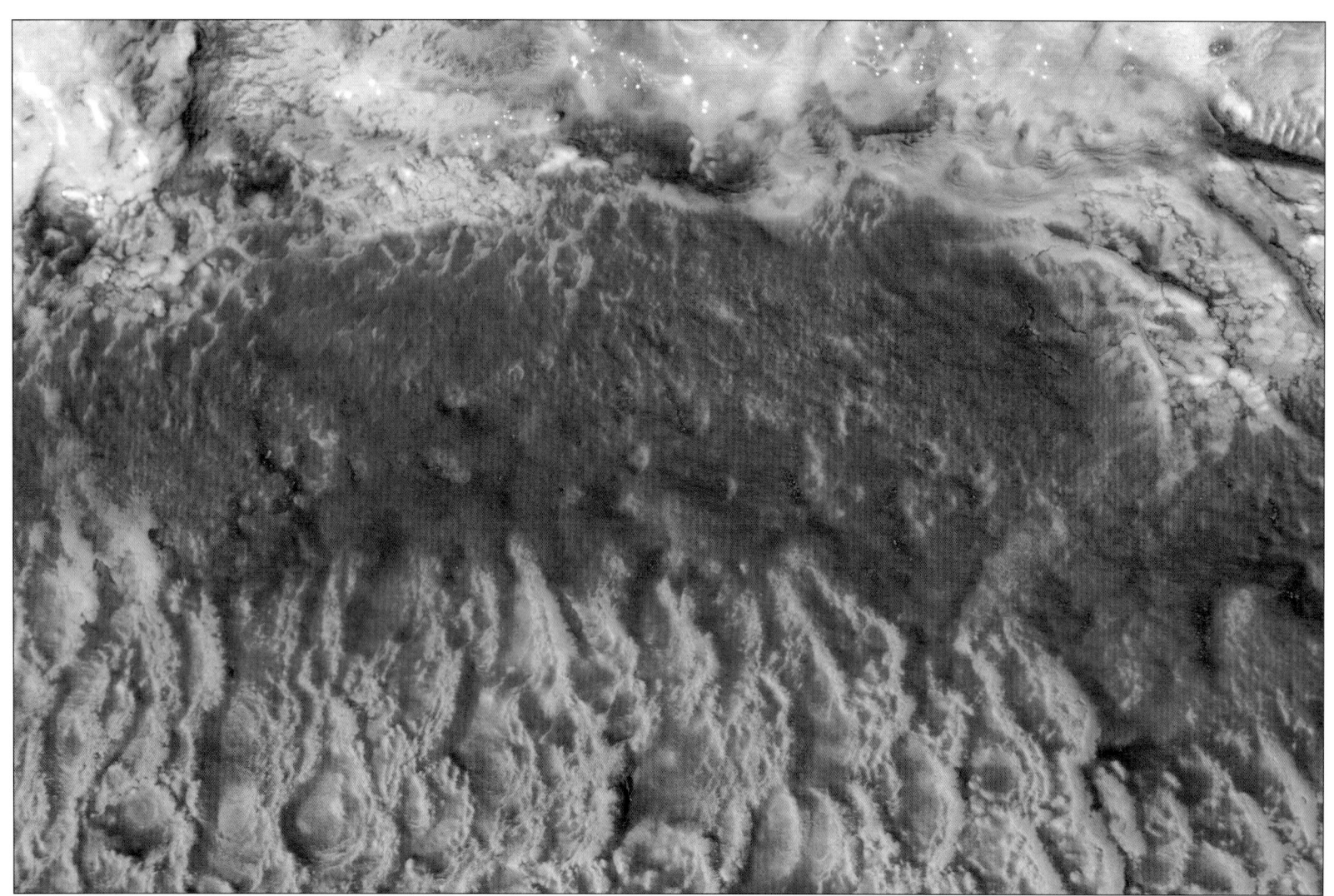

Deposits on Emerald Terrace, Orakei Korako

Te Kapua or the Golden Fleece, Orakei Korako

Kohua Poharu mud pools, Orakei Korako

Ruatapu or Sacred Cave, Orakei Korako

Wairakei

If a pungent odour is synonymous with Rotorua, it is the billowing steam of geothermal fields that gives the Wairakei region its identity. Wairakei, 75 kilometres south of Rotorua and 10 kilometres north of Taupo, is the awesome site of New Zealand's largest geothermal power installation. The combination of Wairakei and six other North Island fields ensures New Zealand is regarded as one of the largest producers of geothermal energy in the world.

Steam is obtained by drilling, often to a depth of 600 metres, into the vast underground reserves of hot water. The sudden release of the water causes it to boil and produce steam. At well-heads the hot water is separated from the steam and 'dry' steam is piped to the generating station on the banks of the Waikato River.

About 3 kilometres north of the township at Taupo the volatility of the Craters of the Moon Thermal Area, 'Karapiti', can be attributed to wells sunk during the late 1950s and 1960s to utilise the local store of underground thermal energy. The subsequent lowering of the water table had an adverse effect on the behaviour of local geysers and hot springs, yet at the same time generated greater amounts of steam. The Karapiti craters became more active as a result, while the geysers of Wairakei unfortunately lost much of their vigour and impact. Principal features of the area are a large and awesome mud pit, and the Karapiti Blowhole, which was once the most powerful fumarole in the Taupo Volcanic Zone. It is still a site of appreciable force and noise.

The Wairakei Thermal Valley lies to the immediate north of the Wairakei Geothermal Power Station. This small valley has lost much of its vigour and impact since the power station development but it still contains silica terraces, small mud pools and steaming ground. Strangely, the water in the Wairakei Stream is cold, despite the heat of the surrounding land.

Lookout view over the Craters of the Moon, Wairakei

Vents on the western side, Craters of the Moon

Central area, Craters of the Moon

Mud crater, Craters of the Moon

Pools in the mud crater, Craters of the Moon

Geothermal fields, Wairakei

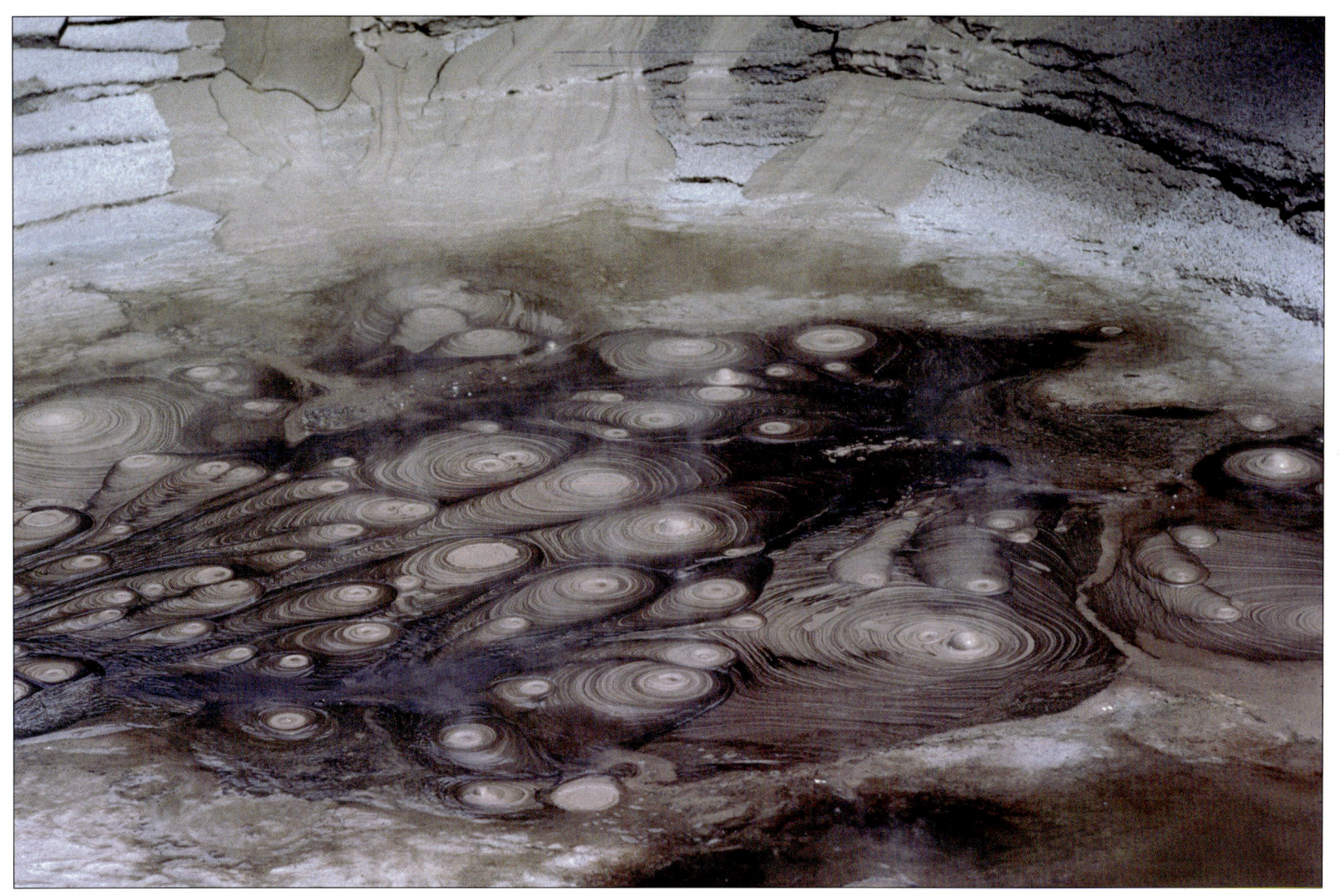

Pools in the mud crater, Craters of the Moon

Geothermal fields, Wairakei

Geothermal fields, Wairakei

Tongariro National Park

The three peaks of Tongariro National Park – Ruapehu, Ngauruhoe and Tongariro – rising dramatically from a surrounding plateau of tussock and semi-desert are the potentially violent remnants of two million years of volcanism.

For many centuries before the arrival of Europeans, the mountains of Tongariro were regarded as sacred by the Taupo tribe of Tuwharetoa. In 1887 the tribal chief Te Heuheu Tukino donated the mountains to the New Zealand Government with the expressed wish that they be maintained 'for the purposes of a national park'. By taking this action Tukino hoped to prevent tribal disputes, European exploitation, and the desecration of sacred sites.

The establishment of Tongariro National Park in 1894 was made possible by this generous 'deed of gift'. All land within a radius of 1.6 kilometres of the peak was affected. The original 2630 hectares were gazetted in 1907 and New Zealand's first national park was created. Since then the park has been enlarged to 75 250 hectares, which includes a separate section to the north enclosing Mt Pihanga and the tranquil Lake Rotopounamu.

At 2806 metres above sea level, Ruapehu is the highest landmark in the park and the highest mountain in the North Island. There are six glaciers on its slopes and two craters at the summit. One of these, Crater Lake, is perpetually warmed by volcanic steam. The eruption of Ruapehu on Christmas Eve 1953 indicated that the mountain could have its lethal moments. A great lahar or mudflow eventuated, which destroyed the Tangiwai rail-bridge, resulting in a train wreck that cost 151 lives.

There were further spectacular eruptions on Mt Ruapehu during 1995–1996 causing the closure of access to its slopes on two occasions and the installation of the world's first 'Volcano-Cam'. The most recent eruption occurred in October 2006 creating a 200-metre water plume and 6-metre waves in the crater lake. The crater's weakened tephra dam burst in March 2007 sending a lahar of mud, rock and water down the mountainside. An early warning system and strengthened riverbanks averted both serious damage and loss of life.

Ngauruhoe, at 2299 metres, was created by an accumulation of debris over 2500 years to form a classic, cone-shaped volcano. Although Ngauruhoe is actually part of the Tongariro vent system it is nonetheless regarded as a separate mountain because of its activity and prominence. In 1954 Ngauruhoe erupted violently. Lava was hurled some 300 metres into the air and 5 million cubic metres of lava flowed down the western side, leaving great heaps of scoria up to 20 metres thick.

Mt Ngauruhoe in late spring

Ketetahi Hot Springs, Mt Tongariro

Mini terrace, Ketetahi Hot Springs, Mt Tongariro

Looking across the South Crater of Mt Tongariro to Mt Ngauruhoe

Central Crater, Mt Tongariro

Emerald Lakes, Mt Tongariro

Blue Lake, Mt Tongariro

Red Crater on Mt Tongariro with Mt Ngauruhoe in the background

Red Crater, Mt Tongariro

Cloud formation over Mt Ngauruhoe

Aerial view of melting snow on Mt Ngauruhoe

Aerial view of Crater Lake, Mt Ruapehu in late spring

Crater Lake, Mt Ruapehu in summer

View from Dome Ridge, Mt Ruapehu

Descent from Mt Ruapehu

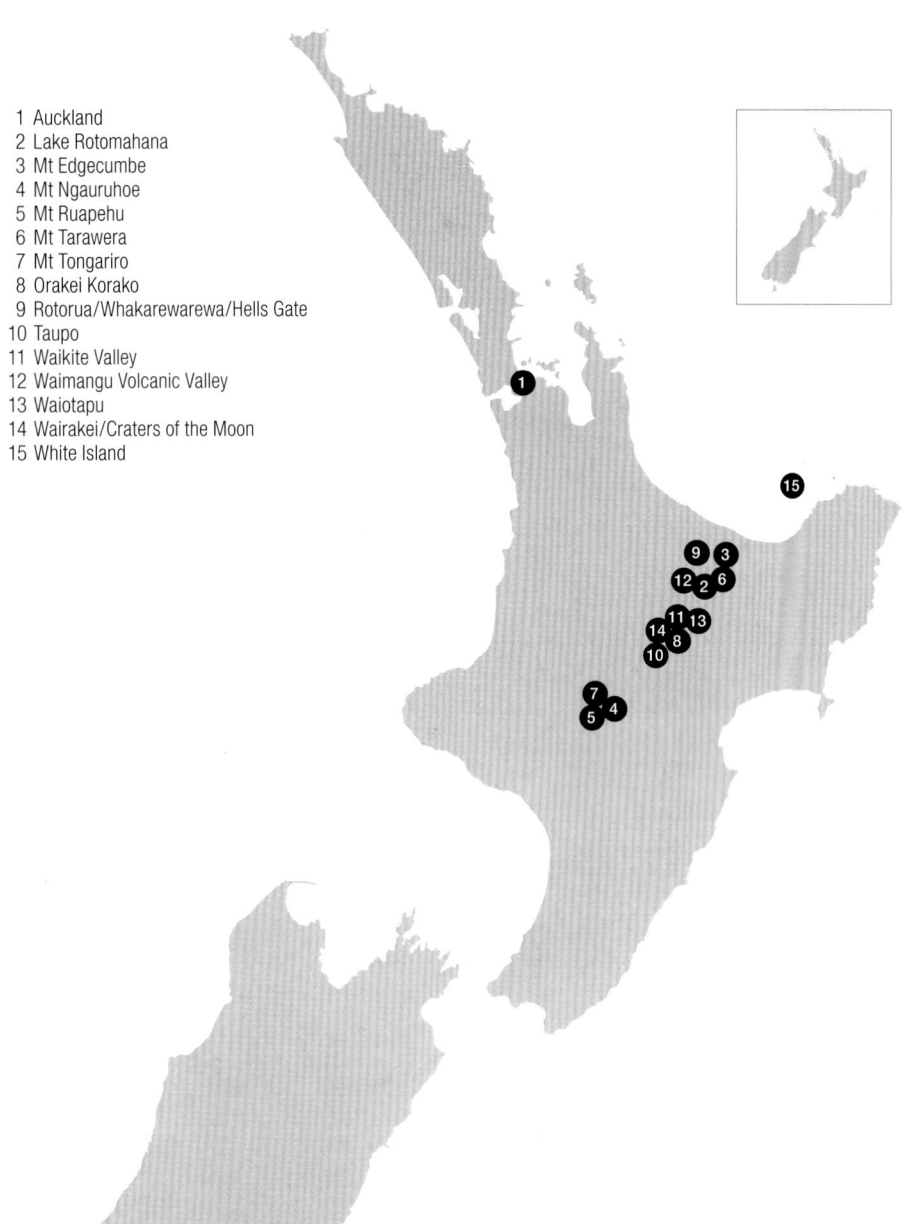

1 Auckland
2 Lake Rotomahana
3 Mt Edgecumbe
4 Mt Ngauruhoe
5 Mt Ruapehu
6 Mt Tarawera
7 Mt Tongariro
8 Orakei Korako
9 Rotorua/Whakarewarewa/Hells Gate
10 Taupo
11 Waikite Valley
12 Waimangu Volcanic Valley
13 Waiotapu
14 Wairakei/Craters of the Moon
15 White Island

VIKING
Published by the Penguin Group
Penguin Group (NZ), 67 Apollo Drive, Rosedale,
Auckland 0632, New Zealand (a division of Pearson New Zealand Ltd.)
Penguin Group (USA) Inc., 375 Hudson Street,
New York, New York 10014, USA
Penguin Group (Canada), 90 Eglinton Avenue East, Suite 700, Toronto,
Ontario, M4P 2Y3, Canada (a division of Pearson Penguin Canada Inc.)
Penguin Books Ltd., 80 Strand, London, WC2R 0RL, England
Penguin Ireland, 25 St Stephen's Green,
Dublin 2, Ireland (a division of Penguin Books Ltd.)
Penguin Group (Australia), 250 Camberwell Road, Camberwell,
Victoria 3124, Australia (a division of Pearson Australia Group Pty Ltd.)
Penguin Books India Pvt Ltd., 11, Community Centre,
Panchsheel Park, New Delhi – 110 017, India
Penguin Books (South Africa) (Pty) Ltd., 24 Sturdee Avenue,
Rosebank, Johannesburg 2196, South Africa

Penguin Books Ltd., Registered Offices: 80 Strand, London, WC2R 0RL, England

First published in
1 3 5 7 9 10 8 6 4 2

Copyright © text Trevern and Anna Dawes, 2007
Copyright © photography Trevern and Anna Dawes, 2007

The right of Trevern and Anna Dawes to be identified as the author of this work in terms
of section 96 of the Copyright Act 1994 is hereby asserted.

Designed and typeset by Adrienne Burn
Prepress by Image Centre Ltd.
Printed by Everbest Printing Co. Ltd., China

ISBN: 978 0 67 007162 3

A catalogue record for this book is available
from the National Library of New Zealand.

www.penguin.co.nz

Acknowledgements to:
PeeJay White Island Tours
Charlie Feast of Mt Tarawera NZ Ltd.
Tourism New Zealand
Managements of Te Puia, Hells Gate, Waimangu, Waiotapu,
Orakei Korako and Craters of the Moon